T0072497

Brown Round Bread Sandwich

SHERRY BABETTE

Order this book online at www.trafford.com
or email orders@trafford.com

Most Trafford titles are also available at major online book retailers.

Print information available on the last page.

ISBN: 978-1-4907-8785-5 (sc)
ISBN: 978-1-4907-8786-2 (e)

Library of Congress Control Number: 2018937828

Trafford rev. 03/22/2018

Trafford
PUBLISHING®   www.trafford.com
North America & international
toll-free: 1 888 232 4444 (USA & Canada)
fax: 812 355 4082

ACKNOWLEDGEMENTS

Thank you for the opportunity of a Rebirth! I am grateful for the newness that life has to offer. Old friends, new friends, family and life experiences have continued to be my best teachers. Thank you all! Life is FASCINATING!

Special thanks to Maya Turpyn for my beautiful cover. My husband/photographer, Mr. Maddox, thank you for your digital imaging skills and wonderful support. Mike Notes and Nadirah Muhammad, thank you.

Wait! Before You Get Started...

I am so happy that you, _____,
(Insert Name Here)

are reading <u>Brown Round Bread Sandwich</u>. But before you get started, I would like to tell you a few things. Depending on what grade you're in, you might find a few of the words in this book a little challenging. So, I have decided to show you many of those words before you start reading! I suggest that you look over the list. If you see words that you don't know, you can look them up, and write down the meanings beside them. That way, you'll have access to the definitions as you are reading. You may still have to look a few words up, but I left some blank lines for you to write them down with your other vocabulary! And if you know all the words already, practice spelling them backwards in Swahili. Just kidding!

After you finish reading each chapter, there will be some questions that I'm challenging you to answer. If you have difficulty, it's okay to ask for help. I always have to ask Ishaq for help. Huh, what? Who's Ishaq? Oh, don't worry. After you look over your word list, you'll meet him.

Once you're done reading the story, there are a few more exercises for you to complete. These exercises will help you with your spelling, writing, and using your words in context. Finally, there are additional pages entitled "Notes", where you can write your thoughts or create diagrams, maps, and other visual aids.

That's all for now. Happy reading!

Words to Know

Accessories (Ch 8) – _____

_____

Affirmation (Ch 9) – _____

_____

Arabian Peninsula (Ch 8) – _____

_____

Aspect (Ch 9) – _____

_____

Authentic (Ch 8) – _____

_____

Awkward (Ch 11) – _____

_____

Bigotry (Ch 8) – _____

_____

Bizarre (Ch 11) – _____

_____

Boomerang (Ch 8) – _____

_____

Confident (Ch 9) – _____

_____

Contributed (Ch 8) – _____
_____

Culinary arts (Ch 8) – _____
_____

Culture (Ch 3) – _____
_____

Curtsey (Ch 8) – _____
_____

Customs (Ch 7) – _____
_____

Diplomat (Ch 7) – _____
_____

Diversity (Ch 6) – _____
_____

Djembe (Ch 11) – _____
_____

Enthusiastic (Ch 8) – _____
_____

Entrepreneur (Ch 11) – _____
_____

Exhibition (Ch 8) – _____
_____

Falafel (Ch 3) – _____

_____

Gesture (Ch 5) – _____

_____

Gouda cheese (Ch 7) – _____

_____

Gyro (Ch 3) – _____

_____

Hesitated (Ch 6) – _____

_____

Humiliated (Ch 4) – _____

_____

Hummus (Ch 7) – _____

_____

Import (Ch 7) – _____

_____

International (Ch 6) – _____

_____

Interstate (Ch 6) – _____

_____

Inventory (Ch 8) – _____

_____

Jeering (Ch 10) - _____

_____

Mañana (Spanish) (Ch 6) - _____

_____

Manufactured (Ch 7) - _____

_____

Mesh (Ch 4) - _____

_____

Mode (Ch 9) - _____

_____

Mudra (Ch 11) - _____

_____

Oral (Ch 9) - _____

_____

Peculiar (Ch 2) - _____

_____

Phenomenal (Ch 8) - _____

_____

Pita (Ch 3) - _____

_____

Plantains (Ch 7) - _____

_____

Pluralism (Ch 8) - _____

_____

Proprietor (Ch 8) - _____

_____

Rotate (Ch 8) - _____

_____

Sincere (Ch 10) - _____

_____

Stammer (Ch 4) - _____

_____

Stats (short for statistics) (Ch 9) - _____

_____

Tabouli salad (Ch 7) - _____

_____

Technique (Ch 11) - _____

_____

Traditional (Ch 8) - _____

_____

Unison (Ch 3) - _____

_____

The United Nations (U.N.) (Ch 6) - _____

_____

Varsity jacket (Ch 4) - _____

_____

Yoga (Ch 11) - _____

_____

_____

_____

_____

_____

_____

_____

_____

_____

_____

_____

_____

_____

_____

_____

_____

!

My name is Ish, short for Ishaq, and I'm 9 years old. Today I'm feeling pretty good, but for a while things were kind of rough for me. I started a new school because my mom and I moved here, from a totally different state, a few months ago. I still don't know what was so bad about where we lived, I had a great time living with my grandparents, uncle, and his dog, Harlem. But Mom said something about more space, cleaner air, better schools, a better job, blah, blah, blah. I never really paid attention to her when she discussed the move because I hated the whole idea. It really stunk! I knew I'd miss my family back home.

Sure, we do have our own place to stay now, and there is a really cool playground in this neighborhood, but I felt like I was here all alone. Mom had a couple of her best college friends here, but who did I have? I didn't have my best friends. I didn't have my favorite Uncle Mike, who is 22! And I didn't have my favorite cousins, Nigel and Ari, who were born on the same day as me. It was just me and Mom in a bigger house, where we each had plenty of our own space. To make myself feel better I'd think, "at least there will be enough room for the family when they come to visit."

Mom really tried to help me make new friends, but most of the people she knew only had daughters my age. "Why is the world filled with girls?" I would ask myself that question over and over. I mean I didn't know any nine year old boys that played with girls.

Most of the time, I would ride my bike to the playground and shoot around at the basketball courts all alone. Mom came sometimes, and we would have fun. But when a group of guys rode by on their bikes, I'd get embarrassed and wish she'd stayed home unpacking. They didn't even try to play with me, and I bet they got a good laugh. What fourth grader plays ball with his mom, even if she is good?

Let me tell you about the day when things really got bad.

What Do You Think About Chapter 1?

Why didn't Ishaq want to move to a new state?

_____

_____

_____

_____

Is it okay for children to have fun with their parents, or should parents stick to telling children what to do?

_____

_____

_____

_____

Would you be willing to move to a new state if it meant having better opportunities or would you prefer to stay close to your family?

_____

_____

_____

_____

2

"Alright class, take your seats, and give us your attention. My name is Mrs. Elliot, and I am your fourth grade teacher. Welcome to a new year!"

"Hello class! My name is Ms. Iesha Arroyo, and I'm your student teacher. I'm in college, and I'll be assisting and teaching along with Mrs. Elliot until December. You can call me Ms. Iesha or Ms. Arroyo."

It seemed like all of the girls had rehearsed when they all said, "We like Ms. Iesha!" Then they started discussing how pretty she was and how they liked her braids.

"Is there anyone who is new to Bayside Elementary?" Mrs. Elliot asked.

"Oh great, here it comes," I thought. I had to put myself in the line of fire. I looked around, but to my surprise, there were 11 other hands up. I added mine to the count. All of the new students looked grateful that they were not alone. In fact, we made up half of the class! And then I realized I knew two of the old students, Amirah and Sade.

Amirah is one of Sade's friends, and Sade lives around the corner from our house. Her mom is my mom's college friend, Monique. I call her Aunt Nicky, and Sade calls my mom Auntie Sherry. We have to call our mom's best friends "aunt" because they think it's more personal than "Ms. or Mrs." since they are close like sisters. Aunt Nicky is married to Uncle Chris. I can't say Aunt Nicky and Mr. Chris! Before we moved, Aunt Nicky and Mom spoke on the phone every single day. She is the one who helped us move down here. Maybe I should be angry with Aunt Nicky instead of Mom.

"Now, I would like for all of the students who attended Bayside last year to stand up and walk to the front of the class. I was once a new student, and my teacher made me stand all alone to introduce myself. I nearly fainted!"

Mrs. Elliot acted like she was fainting. The whole class laughed because she is funny. One by one, students said their names aloud and then sat down.

"Now, I would like for all of the new students to walk to the front of the class to introduce yourselves."

I was seated near the back of the class, so I was the last one to get to the front. It seemed like the whole class watched me as I approached the first row. I shot a nervous glance at Sade and Amirah, and they were smiling.

After the first new student said his name, Mrs. Elliot did something peculiar and started asking him questions. *"So where are you from? Is your family military? Do you have any siblings? What is your hobby?......"*

When it was my turn, I wasn't even nervous anymore. I said that I liked playing basketball and art. Then she asked me what I found most difficult in school. I said I hated math, and the whole class cracked up, except for three girls, who looked shocked.

What Do You Think About Chapter 2?

How did Mrs. Elliot make it easier for the new students to introduce themselves?

_____

_____

_____

_____

Have you ever changed schools? If so, do you have a best friend that you had to leave behind? If not, has one of your friends ever left you behind because they had to move?

_____

_____

_____

_____

_____

_____

_____

_____

3

By lunchtime, I had already made four new friends. We agreed to be a team at recess. I couldn't wait to play basketball, but first I had to eat. I was starving! Mom hates it when I say I'm starving. She starts lecturing me about all of the hungry children throughout the world who literally have no food to eat.

We were dismissed to the cafeteria, so I followed everyone down the corridor. My new friends got on the food line, while I went to the table that had our room number hanging over it. I have been bringing my own lunch to school since kindergarten because I hate school lunch. Sade was already sitting down, taking her lunch out of her bag. She was talking with Amirah and four other girls, Ciara, Layla, Stephanie, and Madison.

"So Ishaq, how do you like it here? Is this school better than your last school? And how come you don't like math?" Layla asked. She was looking at me like she was the school reporter or something. Was she serious? I had only been there for three and a half hours.

With a very serious look on her face, Ciara added, "Well, I sure hope you like technology, because I would be highly offended if you didn't. I'm a big proponent of maker spaces."

It was pretty obvious that they were going to make the honor roll. Anyway, I answered, "Call me Ish; I guess Bayside's okay; long division confuses me; and actually, maker spaces are pretty cool."

"If we call you Ish, can we make a wish?" Madison asked. Then they all started laughing. Girls... I just shook my head and got my lunch out. I hadn't even asked Mom what she had packed.

I pulled out my snacks first. Two juice boxes, a package of cheese crackers and some green grapes. Not bad. Then I pulled out my sandwich container. I wasn't even looking in the lunch bag. I was paying attention to the guys coming over because I hated being left alone with those silly girls. They came over with some of the other guys in the class that I could already tell would give me some trouble. They had been making snide remarks as the new students spoke in class earlier.

"So Ishaq, how good are you at balling?"

As Jake asked me that question, I realized that he was kind of tall. I knew because he looked to be a couple of inches taller than me. Mom always says, "You're gonna be tall, just like your Grandpa Joshua." Four more inches and I'll be five feet tall!

"Call him Ish," Stephanie, said interrupting the interrogation.

"Ish rhymes with fish," Jake laughed, and then his smile turned to this weird, turned-up lip look. "Eeww! Dude, what are you eating?"

He spoke really loud, so the next thing I knew, everyone had these strange, disgusted looks on their faces. I looked at my sandwich and wondered what was wrong.

"It's a sandwich. On wheat pita bread," I said. Faces were still looking strange. "What's the matter with you, you never saw pita bread?" I looked at them like they were strange, but suddenly I felt strange.

"That brown, round thing is bread? Excuuuuuse me! But I have never, ever seen brown, round bread before. Ish the fish is eating brown, round bread!" Jake started laughing and everyone else chimed in with him, except for the girls at the table.

"You guys are soooo immature. Pita bread is Middle Eastern and Greek. Haven't you ever heard of a gyro or falafel?" Sade looked really annoyed.

I heard some of the other kids whisper, "I thought he was Black? He looks Black to me. Wait, is African-American and Black the same thing?..."

"Haven't you heard? This is America, not Greece? Who brings a brown, round, Greek bread sandwich to school? Oh, I know, Ish the fish, the Greek Geek! Is that your boyfriend chubby girl?" Now Jake was snapping on Sade.

"Don't call her fat!" Layla and Stephanie spoke in unison.

"Look, Snake, uh, I mean Jake, haven't you ever been any place to eat besides a burger place. Don't you have any culture?" As I spoke to Jake, I could feel my temper boiling, but Sade chuckled a little.

"Hey, I don't need culture. I'm an American, and I eat American food like frankfurters, tacos, meatballs and spaghetti, and egg rolls. Greek-Geek,

Fishy Ishy. What could you possibly know about balling? I bet you can't even swish!" Jake high-fived one of the guys that I thought was on my side.

Boy, were they clueless. But I knew it. I knew my first day would stink. Everyone finished their lunches and talked to one another. No one spoke to me.

What Do You Think About Chapter 3?

Do you think that Ishaq would have still been teased about his sandwich even if he was not new at his school?

_____

_____

_____

_____

Have you ever been teased because you were somehow different or new to a situation? How did you respond? Did you tell anyone?

_____

_____

_____

_____

_____

_____

_____

_____

Have you ever made fun of anyone who had a different culture, skin tone, or background than you? If, so, how did that make you feel, and do you think that that behavior is acceptable?

_____

_____

_____

_____

_____

_____

_____

_____

What is your favorite food? Is it an American dish? Do you enjoy trying new foods?

_____

_____

_____

_____

_____

4

On my way to recess, I wondered how the game would go. After that incident, I didn't even want to play with anyone. I felt like something was wrong. There was—I hated my stinking school, and I hated my stinking town! I walked towards the courts and threw my lunch bag down near the fence. The guys that I was supposed to play with looked at me nervously. I knew they didn't want me to play with them anymore. And that was fine with me. I decided that once the balls were given out, I would shoot alone. I needed to practice my jump shot anyway; I wanted to try out for the school's team.

I saw a teacher coming from the school with a big mesh sack hanging over his back. I knew it was the recess bag because it was full of balls, frisbees, and jump ropes. I just needed a basketball, so I jogged in his direction. He blew his whistle, and a bunch of children came running over.

"You were first, what do you play?" He had his name stitched onto his varsity jacket, Coach T.

"That brown, round bread, big, round head boy doesn't play, he swims. He's Ish the fish!" Jake shouted from the back of the crowd.

Everyone howled with laughter. Jake had the whole fourth grade laughing at me. I was humiliated. Coach T. blew his whistle. Everyone stopped laughing.

"Jake, you can take a seat for the rest of recess. Not a good start for the school year. Need I give your dad a call?"

"Uh, no sir," Jake stammered. Coach T. looked at me and winked. I grinned a little.

Jake mumbled something, sucked his teeth, and then walked over to the benches. Coach T. looked at me again and asked what I played.

"B-ball, sir."

"You new here?"

"Yes."

"What's your name?"

"Ish, uh, I mean Ishaq."

"Oh, I get it now, name jokes. My nickname was Pickle Juice, and don't ask why! But I got joked plenty when I was coming up. You'll be okay, I promise." He smiled at me, rubbed my head, and then gave me a ball.

I dribbled over to the end court and started shooting around. I dribbled and shot. Shuffled side-to-side, shot. Turned around, shot. Faked a play, shot. Made lay-ups. I tried to block out all the bad stuff that happened in the cafeteria, then I glanced over at Jake. Some of his friends decided to play near him so they could poke fun at people. He pointed over at me. I looked away and shot. Missed. The ball flew over the backboard and onto the grass. Jake and his buddies cracked up. I shouldn't have shifted my focus. The ball rolled over by Sade and her friends.

"Everybody's not messy like Jake and his friends you know." Sade picked the ball up and passed it to me. The ball came straight to my hands, she knew how to pass! She smiled, and I kind of smiled back and thanked her. She'd defended me in the lunchroom and knew how to pass a ball. I began thinking that maybe a girl could be cool. And, she wasn't chubby.

What Do You Think About Chapter 4?

Why doesn't anyone want to play with Ishaq?

_____

_____

_____

_____

_____

Why is it important for teachers and school staff to know about conflicts or challenges that students have with each other in school?

_____

_____

_____

_____

_____

Before Sade passed Ishaq the ball at recess, what information from the text can you use to prove Ishaq really never gave Sade a chance to demonstrate that girls and boys can be friends?

_____

_____

_____

_____

_____

Everyone has times when they feel that they're alone. Ishaq decided to play basketball by himself. When you're feeling lonely, what do you do? How does it help you?

_____

_____

_____

_____

_____

_____

_____

_____

5

The rest of the afternoon was okay, I guess. We didn't stay in the classroom much because we had to meet our other teachers. We lined up for our in-school outing. Our first stop was the library and media center. Mrs. Elliot led us in, reminding us that we must remain silent. It was pretty big, bigger than the one at my last school. We also had a male librarian named Mr. Norman. I had never seen a male librarian before. Mr. Norman gave us a tour and showed us how to log onto the computers and find databases for our research assignments.

Then we were off to the gymnasium. It was huge! I had never seen such a large gym in an elementary school. It even had bleachers! I saw Coach T. in the office. Once he heard our class enter, he came out to greet us.

"Welcome back to school guys!"

Madison and Layla cleared their throats.

"Oh, pardon me ladies. Welcome back guys and gals!" The coach tried to speak with a heavy southern accent. He made the gesture of removing a cowboy hat as he bowed to the girls in the classroom. They all laughed. He informed us that this year we would be playing a lot of team sports like volleyball, lacrosse, kickball, soccer, flag football, softball and basketball. Basketball was all I cared about. I mean, I'm good at all that other stuff, but basketball is my favorite. Then Coach T. dropped a bomb on the guys. He said we would also have to jump rope to earn a good grade. The girls all cheered. The boys all moaned. He and Mrs. Elliot talked for a couple of minutes, then he blew his whistle to get our attention and show us where to line up. We couldn't stay long because another class had to come in. As we were leaving, Coach T. got my attention.

"Hey Ishaq, I saw you shooting around at recess. Are you going to try out for the team? I'm the coach."

Coach T. extended me a personal invitation to try out. I couldn't believe it!

"Sure, when are tryouts?" I had to act like it was no big deal.

"Just listen out for the school announcements every morning. I am not sure when the gym will be available. We have a lot of teams this year. Should be sometime in late September."

"You got it." Finally, something was going my way. The other guys looked at one another, then kind of smiled at me. That is, everyone except Jake. Oh well, I didn't care.

After leaving the gym, we visited a few Double Up classrooms. Double Up is where we will go when we need extra practice with reading, math, or other subjects. Our last stop was the main office area. We met the school secretaries, the nurse, counselors, and we even met the Principal, Mr. Petersen. At my last school, we only got to meet the principal when we were in trouble. I met her once. I was grounded for a whole week. After that, I never wanted to meet another principal for the rest of my life!

What Do You Think About Chapter 5?

Is it fair that the boys have to jump rope and the girls have to play flag football in order to earn a good grade?

_____

_____

_____

_____

Why did Coach T. invite Ishaq to try out for the basketball team?

_____

_____

_____

_____

Discuss why it is important to know the school staff? Do you feel comfortable speaking with the staff at your school when you have a problem?

_____

_____

_____

_____

At 2:55 pm, the bell rang, and my first day was over. We had to do a page of math for homework. It didn't look too difficult. I was so relieved I almost said "Thank God!" out loud. I got my backpack and headed for the door. Mrs. Elliot stopped me as I was leaving the class.

"How was your first day Ishaq?"

"I guess it was alright." I just wanted to forget about The Snake.

"A little birdie told me that the guys gave you a hard time at lunch." Mrs. Elliot tried to sound secretive, but I had already seen the birdie speaking to her.

"Layla, right? Ah, it was nothing really. My mom sent the wrong thing for lunch, that's all."

"Ishaq, you wouldn't know this, but this school prides itself on welcoming cultural diversity. We have children here from several parts of the globe. Don't you dare change the way you eat to fit in with the others. I love pita bread and lots of other breads from all over the world. We are going to be having a special international project coming up. You just prepare to do some research on pita bread. See you mañana!" She smiled and let me leave.

When I got outside, I saw Mom waiting with the windows rolled down. One of my favorite old school songs was blasting from the speakers. So embarrassing! I knew she was just trying to be nice and surprise me, but come on! Someone was already sitting in the back seat, but I couldn't tell who it was. As I approached the car, I saw that it was Sade.

"Hey Mom, Sade." I just wanted to get away from the school. A big crowd of fifth graders was standing nearby, and guess who was with them? If you guessed "The Snake", you're right. It seemed like he knew everyone.

"I heard you had a little beef with some cat at school today?" Mom was trying to be cool. She sounded funny, but I held back my laughter. I wasn't exactly in the mood to joke around. Sade looked at me and waited to see my reaction.

"I'm fine Mom."

"Good. Know what I'm sayin'. Cause I didn't want to have to do my thing. Know what I'm sayin'!" She made some martial arts and boxing moves and was trying to talk like the teenagers and rappers. She knows that makes me laugh, but I still didn't crack.

"Mom."

"I'm just sayin', yo. You know I ain't playin, kid. Know what I'm sayin' son?" That did it, we all cracked up laughing.

"Okay, seriously." She just had to know. "Which one is it? Who's messing with my baby?" I knew she was going to try to find out who was picking with me. But it was no big deal. "I just want to see what he looks like." She was not going to move until she knew. "Sade, you show me."

"The guy right there with the short haircut, blue jeans, t-shirt, and basketball sneakers." Sade was really itching to tell her.

"Uh, Sade," Mom hesitated, "I'm glad that it looks like the United Nations over there, but all the guys fit your description. Can you be more specific?"

"Okay. Oh, he just turned around. He's laughing. Ohmygosh! He just looked over here!" Sade was all excited and spoke really fast.

"I see him. Ish, do you want me to call the school? I mean he was so mean to make fun of you and call you all those names."

"Mom! It's not that serious! But why did you have to send me a wheat pita bread sandwich? That was so *not* cool. Did *you* take that for lunch? Did MaMa embarrass *you* with corny lunches? I bet you had *regular* bread sandwiches. I bet you had a *regular* life. You didn't have to move around and go to a new school. You didn't have to leave your WHOLE entire family behind. I hate this place. This is not my home! I want to go back home...To the city!" I felt a lump swelling in my throat. All I could think was, "Please move the car!"

Mom waited a moment, then pulled off. She didn't respond to my outburst. Sade just looked straight ahead and didn't say anything either. Mom switched to the gospel radio station. I just squeezed my eyes shut. I couldn't cry in the car. I had to wait until we got to the house. But we weren't driving towards the house.

She drove a few blocks in a different direction, then we got on the interstate. I was staring out of the window when something happened that is kind of hard to explain. All I know is that I began to see my experience differently. Like, there were so many trees here and the sky seemed so enormous. There were no big buildings blocking my view. I was able to view the sky as if I had never seen it before. It was so blue, and the clouds were really white and fluffy. I could even see the moon, and it was still daytime! As we crossed a bridge, I saw the ocean. There was so much water. It looked like the ocean and the sky were touching. I only saw polluted rivers back where I used to live. I could look of out my window and see right across the river to another city.

Mom exited the highway and followed signs towards the mall. It was gigantic. I wondered if it had a book store like the shopping center back home. I wanted to get the latest issue of my favorite comic book, but only certain stores carried it. We pulled into a parking space. Mom and Sade got out and started walking towards the entrance. I left my backpack in the car, got out, and walked slowly. I heard them chatting about some topics that I'm not interested in. What were we doing here anyway?

What Do You Think About Chapter 6?

What was Ishaq more upset about, moving to a new city or his problems with Jake?

_____

_____

_____

_____

_____

Why did Ishaq's mom refer to the boys waiting in front of the school as the United Nations?

_____

_____

_____

_____

_____

What is unique about the town, city, and state that you live in?

_____

_____

_____

_____

What is special about your neighborhood?

_____

_____

_____

_____

In what region of the country do you live? Do you live near any bodies of water, mountain ranges, or forests? What types of trees and flowers grow where you live?

_____

_____

_____

_____

Have you ever seen the moon during the day? Do you ever pay attention to the sky at night? Discuss the differences between the sky during the day and the sky at night.

Day-_____

_____

_____

_____

_____

_____

Night_____

_____

_____

_____

_____

What pollution challenge is your neighborhood, city, or state faced with? Do you have any good ideas that could help address these challenges?

_____

_____

_____

_____

_____

_____

_____

7

"Ish, catch up. I have something to show you!" I had behaved like a big baby, but Mom acted like nothing was wrong. Something was up.

I walked a little quicker, hoping she wouldn't ask me for my opinion on an outfit, I really hate that. She had Sade, so she didn't need my opinion. They kept walking, and then they stopped in front of a store that appeared to be out of business. "Okay," I thought, "the store moved overnight. Good, now we can go home."

Mom was still standing there, going through her purse like she was looking for something. She pulled out some keys and began unlocking the door of the closed store. The lights came on, and all I saw was a big space filled with packed boxes all over the place.

"Surprise, it's our new All of Everything International Trade Store! You can even order cool stuff from The Mother Land and Asia!" Mom started doing a ceremonial dance from Nigeria.

"Oh great" I said loudly, "now the kids are gonna call me "*the Diplomat*" or something!" I turned to walk over to a pile of boxes, and sat down.

I felt torn. I hated getting teased for being different. But I couldn't help how spiritually and culturally aware I was. Mom raised me this way because her parents are Muslim, yet they know all about and respect different faiths. Because they weren't able to travel when they were younger, my grandparents encouraged their children to travel in order to learn about other customs and see the world. They didn't just play jazz and soul, they also played classical, salsa, calypso and Afro-Cuban music in the house when Mom was growing up. MaMa and PaPa felt that it was important to connect them to their people in other parts of the world. They're the reason why Mom speaks Arabic, French, and Spanish fluently, has traveled everywhere, and loves different foods. I've been eating foods like naan, plantains, tostones, bean pies, hummus, Gouda cheese and tabouli salad ever since I can remember. Mom really loves traditions from different countries and all that junk, but we live in America! Why did she always have to make *me* feel different?

"Look Ish, since when do you care so much about what other people think?" Mom sounded very irritated.

She had every right to get angry. I shouldn't have made that comment about the diplomat. I knew it was her dream to have a business where she could bring the whole world together. She always promised me that once she got her own store, she would let me be in charge of ordering cool products from the anime I watch and video games that I play. A lot of those goods were manufactured in Japan. She even promised to take me to South Korea to see the K-Pop artists that I liked, once she saved enough money.

She had worked really hard to make this store happen. Before we moved here, Mom worked two jobs to save money. When she was off from work, she was on the computer doing research on how to start a business and get licenses to import and sell goods from other countries. She would still help me with my homework and school projects even though she was tired. I knew that she did this all for me. I felt like a jerk chicken sandwich.

I looked at Sade. She rolled her eyes and walked to the back of the store to look around. I glanced at Mom hesitantly. I knew she would have the ticked-off look on her face. I looked into her eyes, and they were shiny. I saw a tear in my mom's eye and her nose was red. I made my mom cry. I walked over and hugged her.

"I'm sorry. I've been selfish for the past couple of months, and I won't complain anymore. Please don't cry."

Mom turned her head to wipe her eyes and blow her nose. Then she faced me, "Look Ish, I'm tired. I've been doing everything in my power to make OUR lives better! I have prayed and worked and sacrificed! I am working really, really hard to make this store a success for US! So either you're going to get on board and show some gratitude, or I'm not hiking with you!

"Um, Mom," I paused, "do you mean 'you're not rocking with me'?"

"Oh. Yeah. You know what I mean!"

When we finished laughing, Mom gave us a quick tour of the store and asked if we would like to give her a hand after school two or three days a week. She had a few weeks before she could open, and a lot had to be done in a little bit of time. And the best part was that she was paying us to help.

"Uh, ye-ah! This is fab-u-lous, I have a job! Thanks Auntie Sherry." Sade hugged Mom and did some little dance as she said fabulous. Then she started talking about the girl junk she would purchase with her allowance.

All I could think about was all the action figures and the basketball gear I would buy. I definitely wanted a Colin Kaepernick t-shirt! Of course, I would save some of my money. MaMa and PaPa always taught me that if I get a dime, I should save a nickel. I hoped that the store would be ready before the basketball season began. We locked up the store and headed home. Before we got to the house, Mom stopped at the supermarket. She said that she'd only be a minute and told us to wait in the car. Sade and I kept discussing all that we would buy since we had new jobs. When Mom came back, she only had one bag in her hand. Sade looked at me. I just turned away and stared at the moon. I said nothing else that night.

What Do You Think About Chapter 7?

Why do you think that Ishaq's mom probably took a "different" kind of lunch to school?

_____

_____

_____

_____

_____

Is Ishaq selfish? Explain your answer.

_____

_____

_____

_____

_____

Have you ever tried to make your parents feel guilty when they were doing something for your own good? Why or why not?

_____

_____

_____

_____

_____

Based on the text, can you infer what Ishaq's mom purchased at the supermarket?

_____

_____

_____

_____

Is there a contradiction between Ish wanting a Colin Kaepernick t-shirt and not wanting to be teased for being different?

_____

_____

_____

_____

_____

_____

_____

_____

8

I couldn't believe it, but I slowly began adjusting to this place. I realized that things were not so bad since I had been keeping myself busy. Tryouts were scheduled five weeks after school started. I practiced every day during recess, and sometimes Coach would give me pointers on how to improve my shot. His favorite line was, "It's all about the discipline and follow-through."

The store was scheduled to open on the Saturday after tryouts. I was so psyched. Sade and I had earned $300.00 each! We worked almost every day after school until Aunt Nicky came to pick us up. Then we'd go to her house to do our homework and have dinner. Mom would get me at about 9:00 at night. By the time we'd get home, we'd both be exhausted. All we could do was shower and fall asleep.

We even worked on the weekends! It was tons of fun because Aunt Nicky and Uncle Chris are web designers and would bring their teenage niece and nephew, Kailah and Nakai, who knew all about social media. They helped Mom with the interior design and gave Aunt Nicky and Uncle Chris feedback to make the store's website cool and relevant. Kailah and Nakai were hashtag geniuses!

Aunt Cecilia and Uncle Maurice would also come to help out. They have identical twin 6-year-old girls, Kaleemah and Karriemah. They're in the first grade at my school. Sometimes I see them in the hallway, but I never know who's who, so I call them both "K". Mom put Sade in charge of arranging some of the inventory that she was interested in, and I was in charge of arranging some of the merchandise according to my own interests. We each got a "K" to help us out. Luckily my "K" always came over to me, so I never had to call her by name.

****

To begin the week of tryouts, Coach T. made an announcement after the regular school announcements were made:

"Good Morning everyone. Happy Monday! I would just like to remind everyone who is trying out for teams or joining any clubs that all coaches and instructors will be speaking with your teachers to make sure that you are completing your assignments and minding your behavior. We have a school code to uphold, and self-discipline is the key to success. We look forward to visiting your classrooms."

Everyone in class sat up straight and put their desks into order once they heard that announcement.

There were so many teams and clubs that were accepting new members. It seemed like there was something for everybody. My old school only had teams for two sports, basketball and soccer. And the boys and girls were on separate teams. At Bayside Elementary, there were co-ed teams for basketball, softball, soccer, tennis, and track. There were even more clubs: drama, music, dance, art, poetry, chess, golf, wildlife, fencing, double-dutch, rock climbing, and culinary arts. The teams and clubs met throughout the whole school year so that students could rotate or switch. At my old school, the teams only met for a few months out of the whole year.

"Thanks Coach T. My class is so well-behaved now." Mrs. Elliot bowed to the loudspeaker. The class giggled. "Okay everybody. Our class is going to be starting our first big project. We are hosting an international festival, and everyone is going to participate. We will research several nations along with their customs and even have a food festival to celebrate all of the wonderful dishes that have contributed to making me a little round!" Mrs. Elliot put her hands on her belly.

Everybody laughed a little harder this time. Mrs. Elliot always joked about things that people would normally make fun of in a cruel way. She speaks to the class about pluralism and the ugliness of bigotry and says that the person who thinks that they are better than others has the most to learn. She also says, "Be the best you you can be!" I really like Mrs. Elliot. Maybe it's because she reminds me of my favorite aunts, Dorothy and Ruby. Then again, she's funny like my big cousin, Madeline. I miss them all.

Anyway, she went on explaining about how the project would be broken down, and then she said that other classes would visit our exhibition. Our class really got excited and started talking about how phenomenal they would make the festival.

Mrs. Elliot put her hand up to get everyone's attention, "Ishaq, do you think that your mom would mind lending us a few pieces from the new store? Ishaq's mom is preparing for the grand opening of the new All of Everything International Trade Store everyone."

"Yes, and I am helping out." Sade stood up and started curtseying like she was a princess or something.

"Oh really? Sade and Ishaq, why don't you come on up and tell us about some of the things that we will find there?" Mrs. Elliot moved her desk to the side so we could stand in front of the class.

"Will there be anything from Greece in the store?" Jake had to get a wisecrack in. Only his friends laughed at his phony accent he used.

"That'll be enough Jake." Mrs. Elliot spoke to Jake in a stern voice.

Layla and Madison sat up straight and tried to look super-interested. I think they even took notes. They're so extra!

"Ishaq, tell us about the products that we might find in the store. I'm sure it'll have some things there that Bayside has never seen before." Her voice was back to normal when she spoke to me.

"Oh, there are lots of cool things there, and there's something for everyone." I overheard Mom saying that to one of the people passing by in the mall.

I heard Jake whisper, "not me", but I continued speaking.

"Actually, every continent except Antarctica is represented, and I'm sure you know why, with there being no human civilizations and all. There are goods, crafts, and products from everywhere! You can find neat artwork from Africa, Asia and South America. We have textiles and prayer rugs from the Arabian Peninsula, and we even have some boomerangs from Australia. Did you know that the Aborigines of Australia used them to hunt with? If you like jewelry, we have authentic, handcrafted turquoise bracelets, necklaces, and rings from the Southwest. We also have other gems and beaded jewelry. There are different foods, spices, and snacks from all over. But the food is packaged because we can't have perishable food there like eggs, vegetables, produce, and stuff. We can only have wrapped, canned, and boxed food. Like British cookies, even though they call cookies 'biscuits' in England. There is even a section for toys from different parts of the world." I spoke like a professional. Working at the store prepared me for making a class presentation!

"And girls," Sade interrupted, "we have the cutest modest wear, tunics and head wraps in the city. But here's the best part, even though it's an international store, we will have the best specialty dolls made right here in America! Can I get a drum roll please?" She took over my presentation!

The girls started beating on the desks while the guys stared in confusion.

"Sasha's Summer Dolls and accessories will be sold there. Five new dolls will be sold at the All of Everything International Trade Store exclusively, for one month, because their creator is friends with Auntie Sherry. Black Empress, Songbird Sioux, Caribbean Princess, Princessa Pacifica, and Latina Majestuosa will be available to us first. Even the big stores won't have what we have!"

Sade just had to bring up those dolls. Layla and Stephanie started clapping and squealing and dancing around in their seats. Amirah stood up, did the Nae Nae around her desk, and sat back down. Ms. Iesha and Mrs. Elliot started doing the old fashioned Running Man. Everyone laughed!

The class seemed excited. I felt kind of important representing my mom's new business. Coach T. came in just as the class was asking us questions. He took my seat near the back of the class. Jake sat up and wiped the smirk from his face.

"Welcome Coach T. The class was just listening to Ishaq and Sade discussing the goods that will soon be available at the new All of Everything International Trade Store in the mall. Ishaq's mom is the proprietor." The what, I wondered? Teachers always use big words when they speak to one another.

"Really, will she be carrying any incense or oils?"

"But of course! I set up the displays myself. My favorite scent is coconut mango." Sade was way more enthusiastic and excited than me.

"Who wants to smell like coconuts and mangos?" Jake snapped at Sade. He couldn't help himself. Coach looked at him, and Jake looked down.

"I apologize Sade." Jake tried to sound like he meant it.

Coach T. resumed talking, "I've been watching those cooking channels lately. There are a couple of thingamajigs that they use in the islands to make some dishes that I want to try to prepare. I can't find them anywhere. Do you thi—"

Miss, "I'm In Charge" cut him off, "Well, luckily for you, we have a thingamajig section just for cooking. Just look near the food section and you might find them with the international utensils and cookware."

"Cool! So when can I go by to check it out?" Coach asked, sounding like he was really paying attention. They pretend to listen, but sometimes I really think that grownups ignore us children.

I jumped in to bring it home, "The big day is Saturday. It's the grand opening, and there will be free food. My Aunt Cecilia's doing the catering, and she'll be making her famous chicken empanadas, vegetable samosas, plantains, cupcakes, and island fruit punch. There will also be free gifts, face painting, henna tattooing, great music, and dancers. Drummers from Senegal and other African nations will be playing. My mom traveled throughout the continent when she was college. Oh, I almost forgot. Jake, just for you, there will also be Greek dancers performing their traditional dances." I felt myself smiling, and I couldn't stop. It was like it was coming from inside of me or something. Oh forget it! It's just hard to explain.

"Thank you Ishaq, I'm sure I'll see you there. You and Sade can give me a tour. What time should I come by?" Coach asked.

Coach T. was coming!

I was about to answer, but Sade beat me! "Well, we open at 10:00. But I highly suggest that you come around noon, because that's when all the fun is scheduled to begin." Oh, wasn't she just the social butterfly?

"I'll be there. Now, I need to check in with the other teachers to make sure that your buddies in the other classes know that we mean business. Oh, and by the way, if you think you want to try out, I suggest you take your vitamins and get a good night's rest!" With that, Coach T. chuckled and walked out of the class.

What Do You Think About Chapter 8?

What kinds of teams/clubs are popular at your school? Are you a member?

_____

_____

_____

_____

Is there a team/club that you would like to see your school offer? Why?

_____

_____

_____

_____

What interesting cultures/countries have you learned about so far this year? What was most interesting about these cultures/countries?

_____

_____

_____

_____

_____

Have you ever tried out for a team or program and was not selected? How did that make you feel? Would you still like to participate in a non-competitive way?

_____

_____

_____

_____

_____

_____

_____

_____

_____

9

All that week during recess, students were practicing for some type of sport. Girls and boys were perfecting their catches, passes, shots, kicks, and hits. Bayside was in serious training mode. Everyone who was trying out for basketball stayed on the courts practicing foul shots and lay ups. Until we knew who made the team, most of us sort of had the attitude that we had to stick together. But Jake called me a name whenever I missed a lay-up. I missed three, and he called me "Beata Pita", the "Brown Bread Bomber" and "Fishy Ishy." I didn't respond to him because last year at basketball camp, the coaches said that the person who talks the most junk on the court has the weakest game and feels threatened by the other players. And even though I had missed three shots, I knew that my game was not weak.

By Wednesday, it seemed like everyone including me had been replaced by robots. No one stopped moving! At school, everyone was excited about trying out or signing up for something. At home, everything was about the store. Time seemed to pass so quickly.

Finally! Friday, my big day for tryouts had arrived. I woke up 15 minutes early just so that I could wipe clean my favorite sneakers. I bought a New York Knicks t-shirt with some of my earnings, and I definitely had to wear it. I needed all of the luck I could get. Mom was up early too. I knew that she was really excited and nervous. All week she had been unable to pick me up because her interviews kept running over schedule. She was trying to hire stock room and sales assistants to work at the store. It was a good thing that she could depend on Aunt Nicky and Aunt Cecilia to pick me up. She promised that on the day of tryouts she would pick me up on time. They were going to be held after school, and that would give her a few extra hours. I wanted Mom to be on time because I wanted her to be the first to know that I made the team.

When I got to school, I saw that other students were representing their favorite teams as well. The girls who weren't trying out were acting all silly, talking about which boys looked the best. But us boys didn't want to be bothered. Serious players had to be focused. I learned that at camp too.

Jake was wearing a Golden State Warriors jersey. He kept quoting all of their team's stats and bragging about how the Knicks hadn't received a championship ring in decades. And that's when I decided that I had enough! I was fed up. I like Steph Curry, but dissing the Knicks was out of the question! I'd been tolerating this dude's junk talk for weeks, and I didn't want to hear it anymore.

"You know what Jake, in a few hours we're going to be trying out for the same team. And *IF you make it,* we'll be on the same team and we'll be forced to play together. So can you just shut your big mouth, and save it for the court? Maybe you will learn a few new moves." I balled up a piece of paper, pretended to dunk on him, and said in my cool voice, "Ish loves to swish."

"Oooooohhhhh!" was all I heard everyone saying. Sade, Layla, Stephanie and Madison all high-fived each other, and a couple of Jake's boys even came over to me and gave me a pound.

"Finally!" Sade said.

Layla yelled, "Can you add, subtract, and multiply that!"

"I knew he had it in him," Madison said as she did some twirly thing with her hand up in the air. Madison knew everything.

The rest of the day was great. I just felt good. I was even okay with my lunch. I knew Mom was very busy, so I didn't even get upset when I saw that I had a wheat pita bread turkey and Swiss sandwich. She had begun packing regular bread for my sandwiches after that first day. I was proud that my mom taught me about people, places, and languages that other folks had never even heard of. I loved pita bread, and if Jake had a problem with that, then too bad. He walked over to the table. I took a big bite of my sandwich and looked him square in his eyes. He just looked away and sat down to eat his lunch.

At recess, I shot around with Brendan and Donte, two classmates who were also trying out. I missed one lay-up, and Jake kept quiet. When we returned to class, Mrs. Elliot reviewed the steps for dividing fractions, gave us a few problems to make sure we fully understood, then surprised us with free time for the rest of the afternoon. Brendan, Donte, and I got on the computer to look at videos of our favorite players' moves.

Before I knew it, the school day was over, it was time for dismissal, and Mrs. Elliot was making an announcement, "Alright class, make sure that you and your partners start narrowing down the information you'll want to include in your five-minute oral presentations on your countries. Make sure you're including a demonstration of an aspect of their tradition, art, geography, economy, or government. You AND your partners are responsible for articulating the information. Start thinking about a dish that represents your nation for the festival, and make sure you complete the next assignment in the math workbook. Oh yeah, and good luck if you're trying out for the basketball team this afternoon. Take it the hoooop!" Mrs. Elliot took a jump shot against the imaginary defense. It was the best day ever!

When the bell rang, the other students who were trying out picked up their bags, and we all headed towards the gym together. I counted everyone, and there were about 60 of us in the gym waiting to try out for a team with 15 spots. 45 people were not going to make it. But I knew that I was going to make it. I was confident because I had practiced, and I was prepared because Mom and I say our prayers and affirmations daily. Coach T. came out of his office and blew his whistle. My stomach flipped.

What Do You Think About Chapter 9?

Is there anyone bullying you or making you feel uncomfortable at school (or outside of school)? Have you told anyone? If not why? If so, have they helped to resolve the situation? Have you ever stood up to a bully?

_____

_____

_____

_____

_____

_____

_____

_____

Have you ever worked hard to achieve a goal? What was the goal and the result?

_____

_____

_____

_____

Think of something that you really want to be good at. Do a little research and list a few of the steps that it would take to become an expert at it:

1) _____

_____

2) _____

_____

3) _____

_____

4) _____

_____

5) _____

_____

A few other teachers in workout gear instructed us to go into the locker rooms to change our clothes. When we returned to the gym, they began separating us to get us stretched and warmed up. Then we heard the whistle.

Everyone stopped speaking to listen for Coach's directions, "Alright, listen up. There are a lot of you here waiting to try out. We're gonna try out in several sessions. Each session will do the same thing. You are welcome to stay after your session has ended, but you must be quiet. No jeering or cheering for the other players. Team spirit and being a good sport is more important than winning."

Coach and the teachers began handing us all blue and green reversible jerseys to wear over our own t-shirts and lined us up into two long lines of thirty. He then made us count off up to 10. Each group of 10 was divided in half. Five had to wear blue, the other five green, and the blues and greens would play one another. The first team to score 15 would win. We had to do lay-up and 3-man weave drills, run a few laps, and shoot free throws. It sounded like a lot to some of the others trying out, but I knew it wouldn't take long.

Jake was one of the tallest guys in the gym. He was in a different group than me, and his group played before mine. But before he tried out, Jake made a lot of wise cracks that Coach didn't hear. He laughed at the few second and third graders that were brave enough to try out. A few of the guys in the first game were good, but I wasn't too concerned. I knew I had the speed and the skill. I was sure that there would be a place for me.

Coach blew his whistle, thanked the first group, and instructed the second group to begin. The second group seemed to be a little rougher, but they were not as aggressive as the third group. Maybe it was because there were more fourth and fifth graders included. But then again, there were these two girls who were sisters, Nadirah, who was a fifth grader, and Alissa, who was also a fourth grader. They teamed up and played "d" against Jake. They each stripped the ball from him and went on to make their lay-ups. A few people cheered for them, even me. Coach T. blew his whistle and gave us a serious look. During their short game, Nadirah outran, out-dribbled, and out-shot her group. She finished her laps first and completed her lay-ups and foul shots effortlessly. Her sister came in second. They were reeeally good, like Venus and Serena. It was obvious that they had made the team. Jake had three rebounds and one assist, but he never scored. He did okay with his lay-ups and free throws, but the 3-man weave was a wreck for all of us.

The fourth and fifth games felt like they took forever, but they finally ended. Then it was my turn. While I was watching the others play, I was fine. But as I walked onto the court, I began feeling a little nervous. Then Coach blew his whistle, and it was on. I scored the first six points, had 3 assists, and grabbed 4 rebounds for the team. I was on fire! The laps were a breeze, and as for the lay-ups and foul shots, I didn't miss one. Then Coach blew his whistle, and tryouts were over. That was it. Everyone ran out on the court and started discussing each session's best and worst plays. Jake walked over to me and gave me the shock of my life. It was an awesome moment!

"You may eat weird food, but you can ball. Maybe I should try one of those funny-looking sandwiches to improve my game." Jake actually gave me a sincere smile as we fist-bumped.

"I'll ask my mom to make you a sandwich on Monday. Mayo or Mustard?"

"Both."

"Oh, now that's disgusting!" I made the "yuck" face, and we started laughing.

We gave each other a high-five and went to gather our belongings. We talked about tryouts until his dad came to get him. I hadn't paid attention to the time, since I was busy talking with some of the others who had not been picked up. I saw more and more parents arriving at the gym and finding their children. Some of them rubbed their children's heads as they walked off. Those guys probably said they didn't think they made the cut. I couldn't wait to tell Mom how well I did. I heard a voice over the loud speaker telling Coach T. he had a phone call. He excused himself from the parent he was speaking with and jogged to his office to answer the phone. Just about all of the parents had arrived. I was waiting along with Brendan. But then his father came. I just kept wishing that Mom would hurry. I knew that I had made it. Then I got scared, because Coach headed out of his office with his things and turned out the lights.

What Do You Think About Chapter 10?

How important is confidence when you are trying to be good at something?

_____

_____

_____

_____

Is it a big deal when a girl beats a boy at a sport? Why?

_____

_____

_____

_____

Why do you think that Jake decided to be a good sport towards Ishaq?

_____

_____

_____

_____

If you were Ishaq, would you have offered to bring Jake lunch? Why?

_____

_____

_____

_____

_____

II

"Well young man, it looks like I will get a sneak peek at the store. Your mom just called to say she was on the way. But I figure with traffic and all, by the time she gets here, the custodians will have you on the sidewalk. So I'm gonna take you to her. Plus, I like that fresh t-shirt you're wearing. The Knicks are my team too. I think I'll get myself a jersey."

"Who's your favorite player?..."

As we talked on the way to the mall, I decided that Coach T. was cool. He had a cool pick-up truck too. He listened to cool music. He didn't even seem like a teacher anymore. We arrived at the mall and saw a sports apparel store as soon as we walked in.

"You think your mom will mind if we stopped here for a second?"

"My mom won't even notice. She's been so busy." Even though Coach was cool, I was still a little disappointed that Mom hadn't shown up.

We went into the store, and Coach went straight to the New York section. He got the jersey, then picked out a plain white t-shirt to wear under it. I suggested he get some new sneakers.

"What are you trying to say about my high tops, they're not hip enough? Yo, homeboy, I'm jiggy."

"Oh no, not you too! My mom always tries to keep up with the new slang. She sounds so ridiculous." I laughed, thinking about the first day of school when Mom picked me up.

"Hey, one day your children will be laughing at you. You'll see." Coach smiled as he pointed his finger warning me.

We had a great time. He let me pick out his new kicks. They were white and had blue stripes that matched his jersey. Coach T. said I made a good shopping buddy. It felt good to be hanging out with a big guy again. My Uncle Mike used to take me along with him when he would go shopping or to the courts to ball. He has even taken me to work with him and his boys at the music studio. I would listen as he produced beats for the tracks that they were working on. Since he was in college and had assignments, he'd take me to the library with him. I would draw or do my work while he did his. Before we moved, he took me to a Big3 tournament game and I got to see Ice Cube! I really miss my Uncle Mike.

By the time we reached the store, Mom was speaking on the phone. She looked really bothered. One hand was on her head, and she kept shaking her head from side to side. Something was wrong. She hung up the phone and stared straight ahead. I don't even think she saw when Coach T. and I entered the store.

"Hi, Mom. What's the matter?" I walked over to her and put my arm through her arm to hug her around the waist.

"Hey Ish. You won't believe how everything has just gone crazy with just two phone calls. Two assistants that I hired to start tomorrow, grand opening day, call me within minutes of each other to tell me that they can't work weekends! THEY CAN'T WORK WEEKENDS! What am I going to do?" She sat down on a large, handcrafted Ghanian djembe drum, and put both hands on her head. Again, she shook her head from side to side. She looked at me, finally noticing Coach with me. She jumped up and tried to seem a little more calm and in control of everything.

"Oh my goodness, oh please excuse me. You're Coach T. I'm Sherry. Thank you so much. Did I cause you any trouble? How much do I owe you for gas? How were tryouts? Ish, did you make the team? I can't stop talking. Ohmygosh. I sound like Sade. Okay, I have to calm down. Just calm down. Must. Calm. Down."

Mom started doing her yoga breathing. She took deep breaths in and out with her eyes closed. It really got awkward.

I looked at Coach and shrugged my shoulders. I had seen Mom use her calming down techniques, but this never happened in front of anyone before. Coach just smiled and gave me the thumbs up sign.

In a very calm voice, Coach began speaking to my mom, "Uh, Sherry, everything will be just fine. How much training does a sales assistant need to work here? A couple of guys that I used to coach are looking for work. They're in college, and I'm sure they would love to work here. I'll shoot them a text to see if they're available to come this evening so you can interview them. And as for tomorrow, I could help out. You just need to show me around."

"You must think that I am the most scatter-brained mother and entrepreneur ever. Oh, how did I get like this? I used to be so organized. Lord, please help me!" More yoga. She took deep breaths and closed her eyes. Her arms were positioned to put her hands into a mudra.

"Look, it's not your fault that your workers bailed on you at the last minute. This is just a challenge, and we all have to face different challenges. Believe me, I know you are a winner. Look at this place! You have put a lot of grind into this store, and one little setback won't stop you. Besides, you still have Ish and Sade." My basketball coach had to coach my mom. It was both bizarre and embarrassing.

"Yeah Mom! Did you forget you already have your best friends to help out tomorrow? After difficulty comes ease. Stop worrying, you know you got this!" *After difficulty comes ease.* I couldn't believe it, but I actually said what MaMa says to me when I'm nervous or afraid. I guess I had matured a little.

Mom's breathing began to slow down. I knew that in a few more moments she would be back to herself. She took one last deep breath.

"Amen. Thank you, Father. Alright, alright. I'm good. Okay, I'm chillin' straight! Hey, I know you're both hungry. Why don't you let me treat you guys to something from the food court? Dessert included." Mom spoke like she was back to herself.

"Mom. It's either straight chillin' or I'm straight. But it is never, ever chillin' straight. Know what I'm sayin' Son!"

We all laughed together and headed out of the store. She locked up, and we were off to get some grub. Each of us ordered something different. Mom had Mexican, Coach had Indian, and I had Greek. As we ate, Mom discussed how she would use Coach in the store the following day. She would have to give him a store t-shirt to work in. Everyone else had theirs already. Coach checked his phone to see if his players had replied to his text. He gave Mom the thumbs up, and said they were on their way.

After we ate, we headed back to the store to finish preparing for the grand opening. The guys arrived, and Mom took them to her office for their interviews. Within ten minutes, she'd offered them both jobs—they were bilingual! I found three t-shirts for Coach and the new staff to wear to work the next day, and I showed him where he should look for his thingamajig.

Then we had a blast listening to old school hip hop as we helped out with some finishing touches. By the time we closed the store, Mom was certain that the grand opening would be a huge success. And the best part of the night was that Coach T. told me that I was the team's shooting guard.

The End

What Do You Think About Chapter 11?

Do you have a parent or favorite older family member/friend who lets you hang out with them? What types of things do you do together?

_____

_____

_____

_____

Do you think that Coach and Ishaq will hang out again?

_____

_____

_____

_____

Make a prediction about the All of Everything International Trade Store.

_____

_____

_____

_____

Figure It Out!

Use your vocabulary list to figure out the words below.

1.   ____ ____ ____ t ____ ____ ____

2.   ____ ____ ____ ____ f ____ ____ ____ ____ ____ e ____

3.   ____ ____ ____ ____ u ____

4.   ____ ____ ____ ____ e ____ ____ ____ ____ ____ ____ r

5.   ____ ____ ____ ____ t ____ ____

6.   ____ ____ ____ ____ ____ ____ g

7.   ____ n ____ ____ ____ ____ ____ ____ ____

8.   ____ r ____ ____ ____ ____ ____ ____ ____ ____

9.   ____ ____ n ____ ____ ____ ____

10.   ____ ____ ____ ____ ____ ____ ____ ____ ____ ____ a ____

11.   ____ ____ s ____ ____ ____ ____

12. ___ ___ ___ ___ ___ ___l

13. ___ ___ ___ ___u ___ ___ ___ ___ ___ ___

14. ___ ___ ___ ___ ___e

15. ___ ___ ___ ___ ___ ___d

16. ___ ___ ___ ___ ___i ___ ___

17. ___e ___ ___ ___ ___ ___ ___ ___

18. ___ ___ ___ ___ ___s ___ ___ ___ ___ ___

19. ___ ___a ___ ___ ___ ___ ___ ___

20. ___ ___ ___ ___ ___ ___q ___ ___

21. ___ ___ ___ ___r ___ ___ ___ ___ ___ ___

Use It in a Sentence....

1. (approach)

_____

_____

2. (culture)

_____

_____

3. (diversity)

_____

_____

4. (enormous)

_____

_____

5. (humiliated)

_____

_____

6. (international)

_____

_____

7. (pita)

_____

_____

8. (proprietor)

_____

_____

9. (stats or statistics)

_____

_____

10. (stern)

_____

_____

11. (traditional)

_____

_____

12. (varsity jacket)

_____

_____

A synonym is a word that has the same or similar meaning as another word.

For example: work ➡ toil, labor, effort

Use a thesaurus to find synonyms for the following words:

Aggressive   _____

Contribute   _____

Enormous   _____

Glance   _____

An antonym is a word that has the opposite meaning of a word.

For example: enter ➡ leave, exit, depart

Use a thesaurus to find antonyms for the following words:

Former   _____

Immature   _____

Stern   _____

Irritate   _____

Common Homonyms

A homonym or homophone is a word that has the same sound as another word, but is spelled differently.

For example: 1) to, too, two 2) air, heir 3) hair, hare

Write the homonyms for the following words:

There _____ _____

Through _____ _____

Where _____ _____

To _____ _____

Ate _____

Capital _____

Eye _____

Fourth _____

Higher _____

Need _____

Principal _____

Son _____

Your _____

NOTES:

NOTES:

NOTES:

NOTES:

NOTES:

NOTES:

NOTES:

Printed in the United States
By Bookmasters